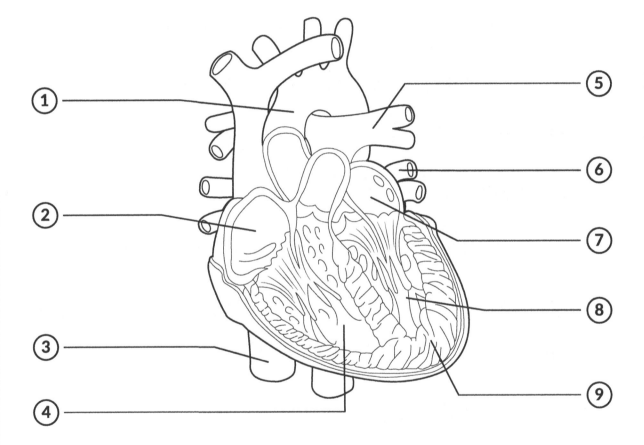

- - Answer - -

(1). Aorta

(2). Right Atrium

(3). Inferior Vena Cava

(4). Right Ventricle

(5). Pulmonary Artery

(6). Pulmonary Vein

(7). Left Atrium

(8). Left Ventricle

(9). Heart Muscle

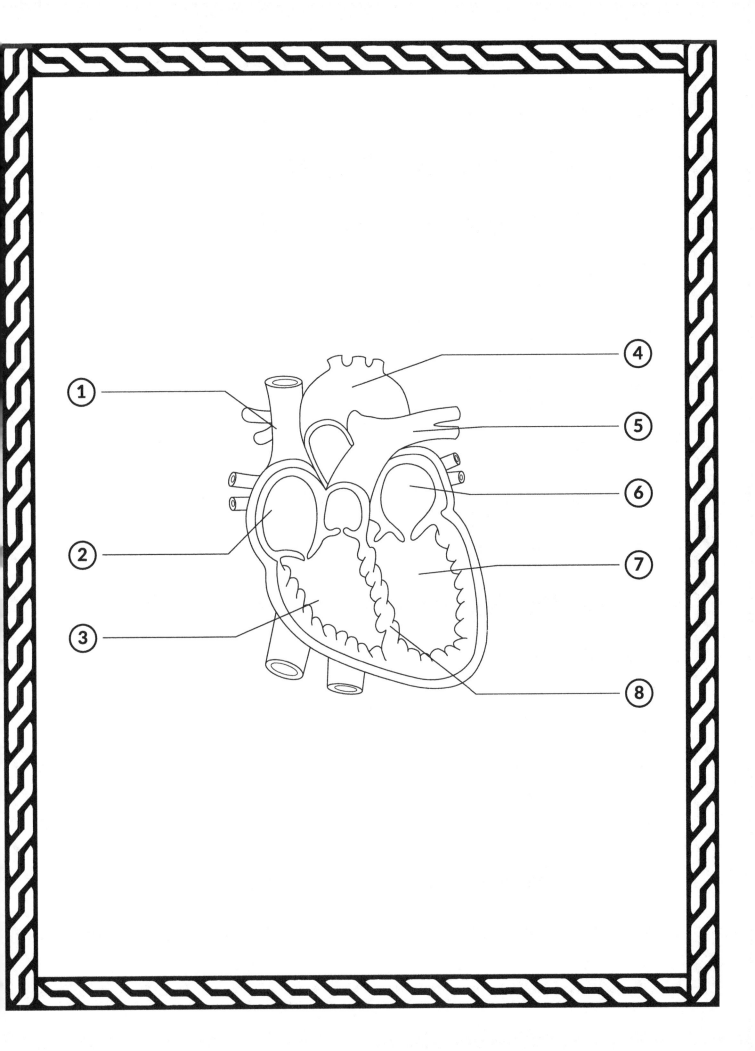

- - Answer - -

(1). **Superior Vena Cava**

(2). **Right Atrium**

(3). **Right Ventricle**

(4). **Superior Vena Cava**

(5). **Pulmonary Artery**

(6). **Left Atrinum**

(7). **Left Ventricle**

(8). **Interventricular Spectum**

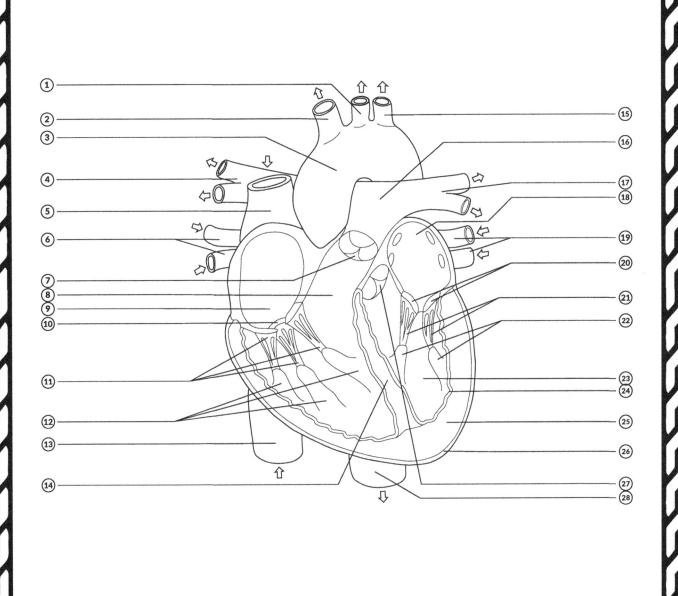

- - Answer - -

(1). Left Common Carotid Artery

(2). Brachiocephalic Artery

(3). Aortic Arch

(4). Pulmonary Artery

(5). Superior Vena Cava

(6). Pulmonary Veins

(7). Pulmonary Semilunar Valve

(8). Right Ventricle

(9). Right Atrium

(10). Tricuspid Valve

(11). Chordae Tendineae

(12). Papillary Muscle

(13). Inferior Vena Cava

(14). Interventricular Septum

(15). Left Subclavian Artery

(16). Pulmonary Trunk

(17). Pulmonary Artery

(18). Left Atrium

(19). Pulmonary Veins

(20). Bicuspid (Mitral) Valve

(21). Chordae Tendineae

(22). Papillary Muscle

(23). Left Ventricle

(24). Endocardium

(25). Myocardium

(26). Epicardium (Visceral Pericardium)

(27). Aortic Semilunar Valve

(28). Aorta

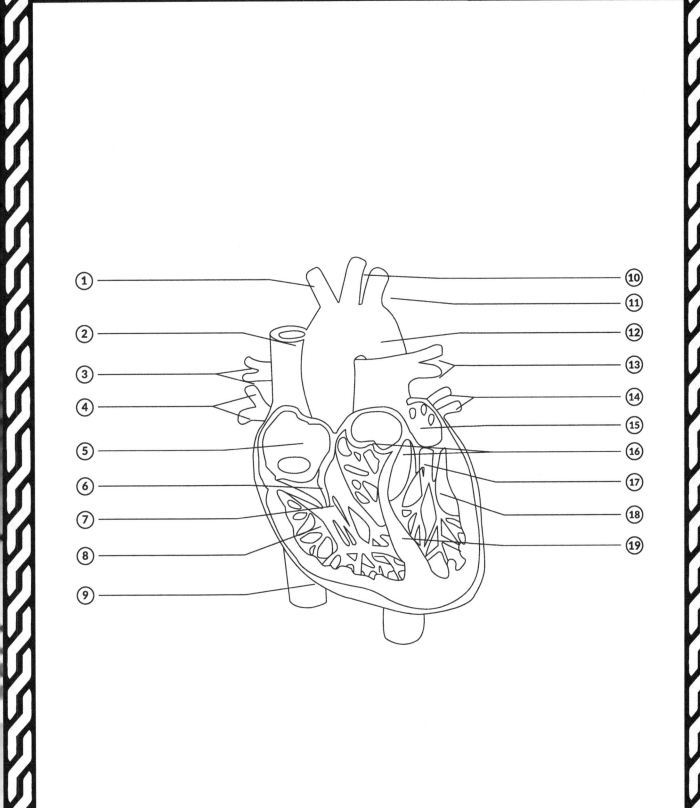

①   ⑩

②   ⑪

③   ⑫

④   ⑬

⑤   ⑭

⑥   ⑮

⑦   ⑯

⑧   ⑰

⑨   ⑱

          ⑲

- - Answer - -

(1). Brachiocephalic Artery

(2). Superior Vena Cava

(3). Right Pulmonary Arteries

(4). Right Pulmonary Veins

(5). Right Atrium

(6). Atrioventricular Tricusoid Valve

(7). Chordae Tendineae

(8). Right Ventricle

(9). Inferior Vena Cava

(10). Left Common Cartoid Artery

(11). Left Subclavian Artery

(12). Aorta

(13). Left Pulmonary Arteries

(14). Left Pulmonary Veins

(15). Left Atrium

(16). Semilunar Valves

(17). Atrioventricular mitral Valve

(18). Left Ventricle

(19). Septum

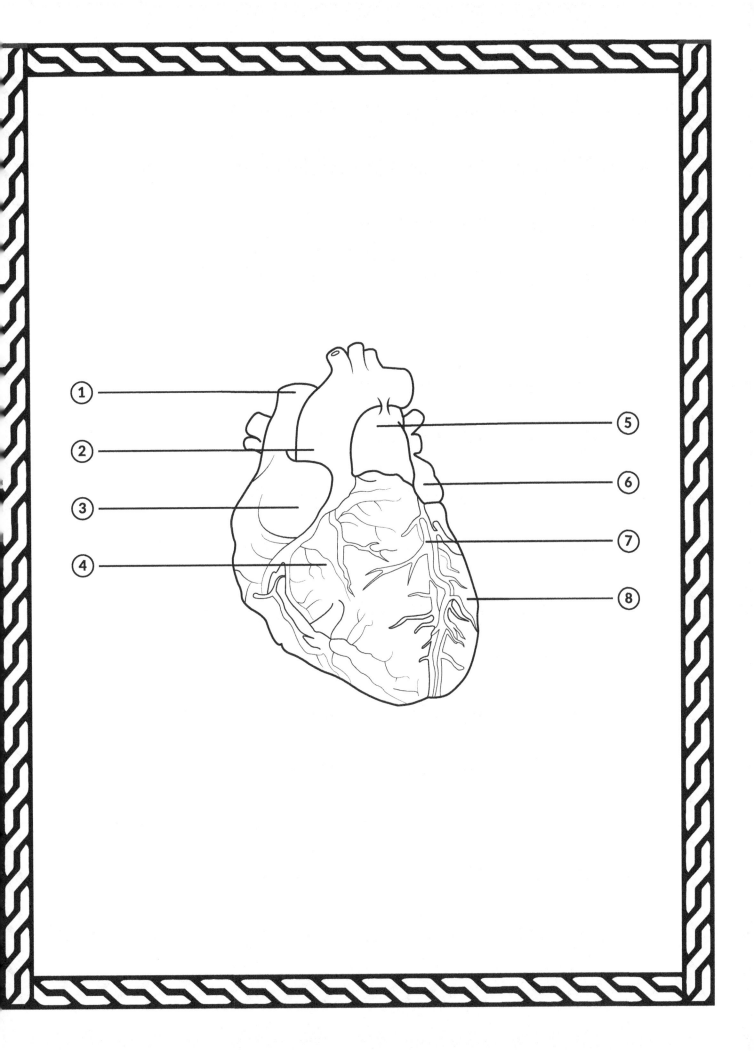

- - Answer - -

(1). Superior Vena Cava

(2). Aorta

(3). Right Atrium

(4). Right Ventricle

(5). Pulmonary Trunk

(6). Aorta

(7). Coronary Vessels

(8). Left Ventricle

- - Answer - -

(1). Superior Vena Cava

(2). Right Atrium

(3). Right Ventricle

(4). Endocardium

(5). Septum

(6). Aorta

(7). Pulmonary Artery

(8). Pulmonary Vein

(9). Left Atrium

(10). Left Ventricle

(11). Myocardium

(12). Pericardium

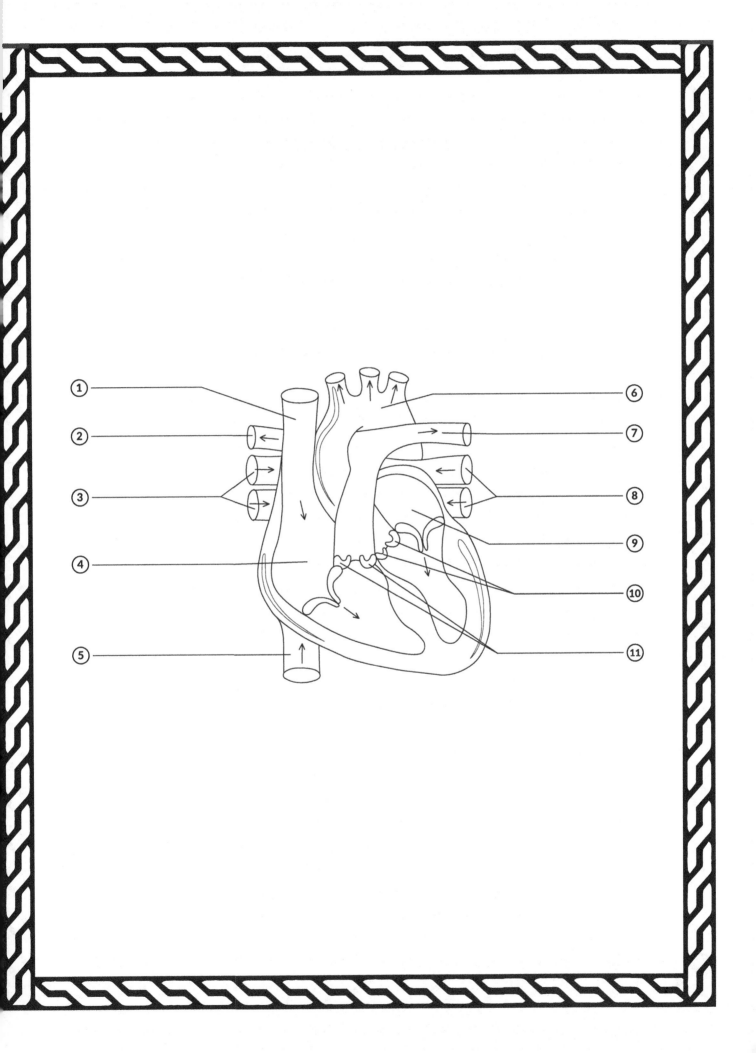

- - Answer - -

(1). Superior Vena Cava

(2). Right Pulmonary Artery

(3). Right Pulmonary Veins

(4). Right Atrium

(5). Inferior Vena Cava

(6). Aorta

(7). Left Pulmonary Artery

(8). Left Pulmonary Veins

(9). Left Atrium

(10). Aortic Semilunar Velve

(11). Pulmonary Semilunar Velve

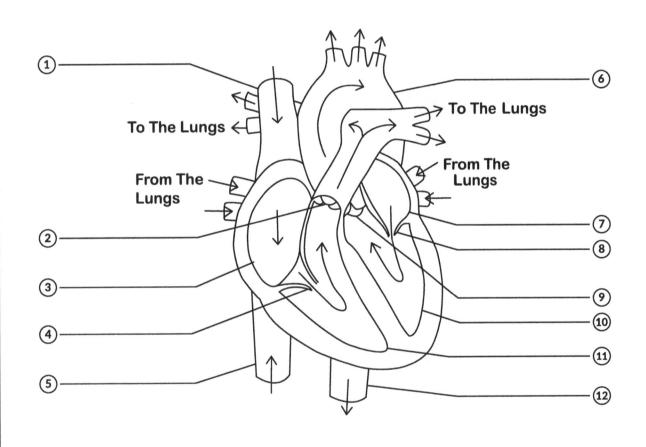

①   ⑥

To The Lungs

To The Lungs

From The
Lungs

From The
Lungs

②   ⑦

                   ⑧

③   ⑨

                   ⑩

④   ⑪

⑤   ⑫

- - Answer - -

(1). Superior Vena Cava

(2). Pulmonary Valve

(3). Right Atrium

(4). Tricuspid Valve

(5). Inferior Vena Cava

(6). Aorta

(7). Left Atrium

(8). Mitral Valve

(9). Aortic Valve

(10). Left Ventricle

(11). Right Ventricle

(12). Descending Aorta

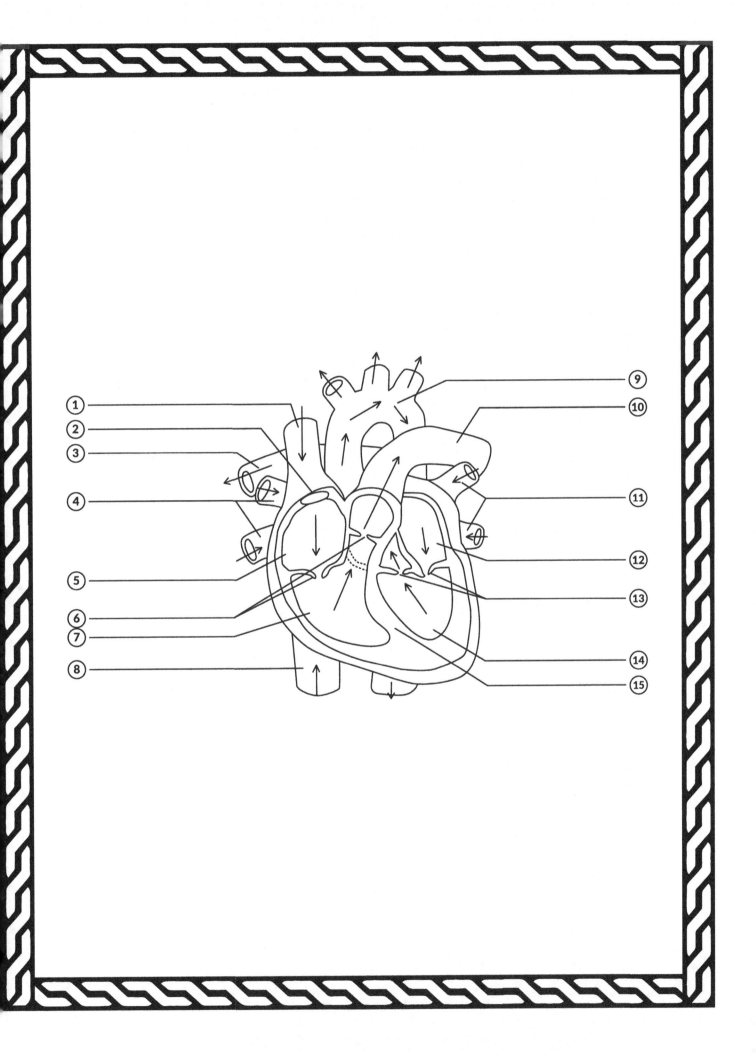

- - Answer - -

(1). Superior Vena Cava   (9). Aorta

(2). Pacemaker   (10). Pulmonary Artery

(3). Pulmonary Artery   (11). Pulmonary Vein

(4). Pulmonary Vein   (12). Left Atrium

(5). Right Atrium   (13). Valves

(6). Valves   (14). Left Ventricle

(7). Right Ventricle   (15). Septum

(8). Inferior Vena Cava

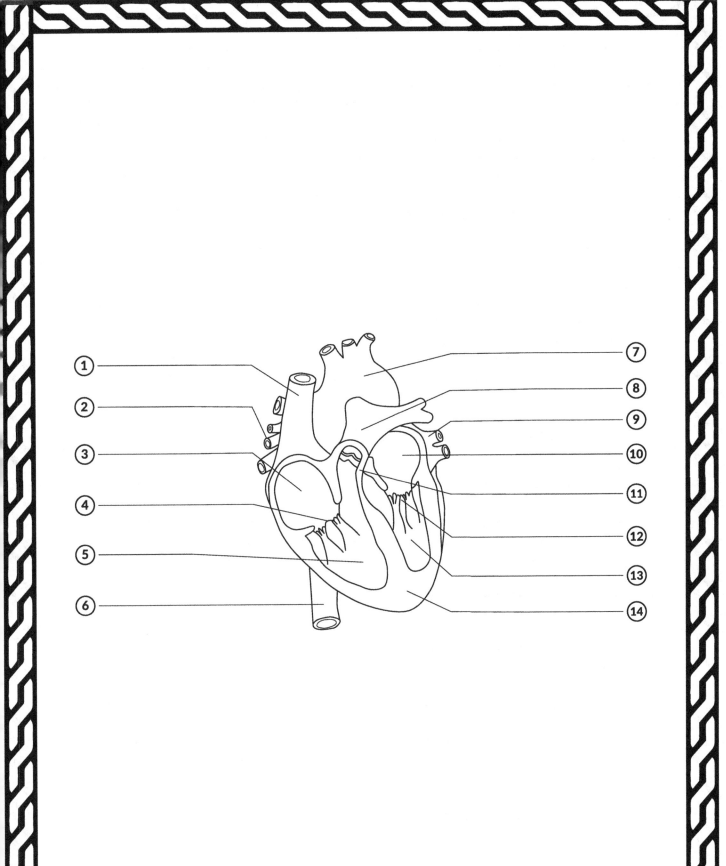

- - Answer - -

(1). **Superior Vena Cava**

(2). **Pulmonary Veins**

(3). **Right Atrium**

(4). **Tricuspid Valve**

(5). **Right Ventricle**

(6). **Inferior Vena Cava**

(7). **Aorta**

(8). **Pulmonary Artery**

(9). **Pulmonary Veins**

(10). **Left Atrium**

(11). **Pulmonary Valve (Or Semi-Lunar Valve)**

(12). **Mitral Valve**

(13). **Left Ventricle**

(14). **Cardiac Muscle**

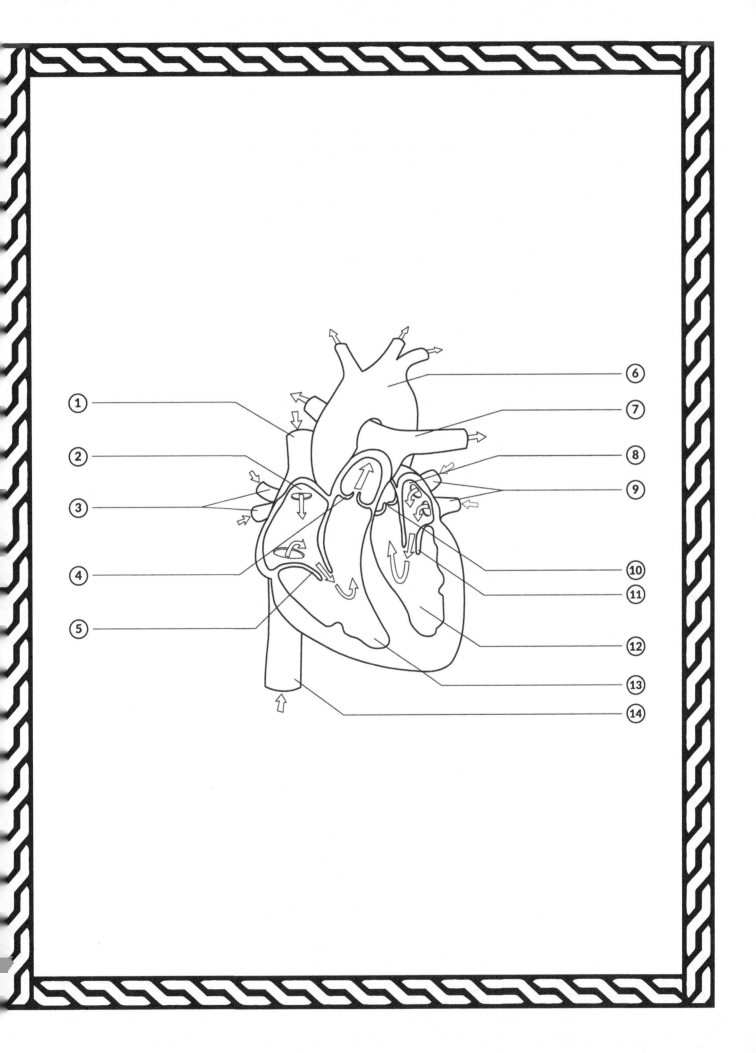

- - Answer - -

(1). Anterior Vena Cava

(2). Right Atrium

(3). Pulmonary Veins

(4). Semiluner Valve

(5). Atrioventricular Valve

(6). Aorta

(7). Pulmonary Artery

(8). Left Atrium

(9). Pulmonary Veins

(10). Semiluner Valve

(11). Atrioventricular Valve

(12). Left Ventricle

(13). Right Ventricle

(14). Posterior Vena Cava

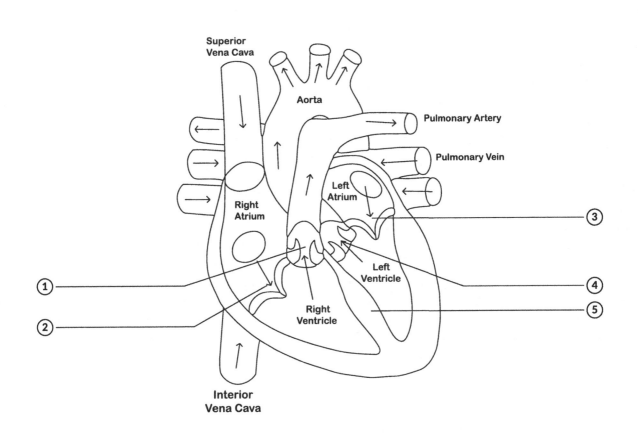

Superior
Vena Cava

Aorta

Pulmonary Artery

Pulmonary Vein

Left
Atrium

Right
Atrium

③

Left
Ventricle

①

④

②

⑤

Right
Ventricle

Interior
Vena Cava

- - Answer - -

(1). Pulmonary Valve

(2). Tricuspid Valve

(3). Mitral Valve

(4). Aortic Valve

(5). Septum

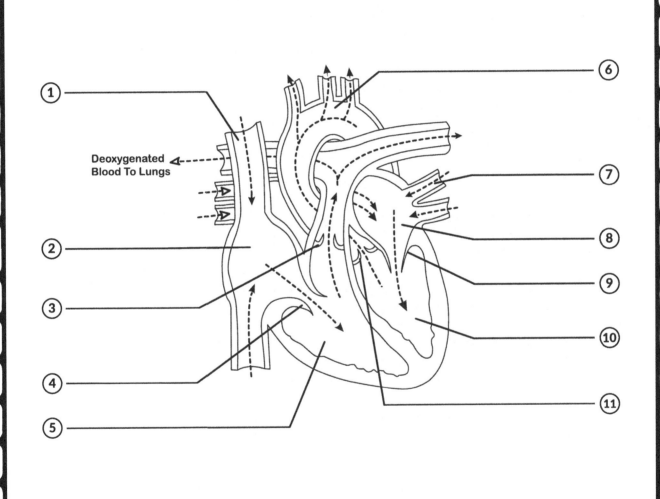

Deoxygenated Blood To Lungs

- - Answer - -

(1). Deoxygenated Blood From Body

(2). Right Aorta

(3). Pulmonary Valve

(4). Tricuspid Valve

(5). Right Ventricle

(6). Oxygenated Blood To Body

(7). Oxygenated Blood From Lungs

(8). Right Aorta

(9). Mitral Valve

(10). Left Ventricle

(11). Aortic Valve

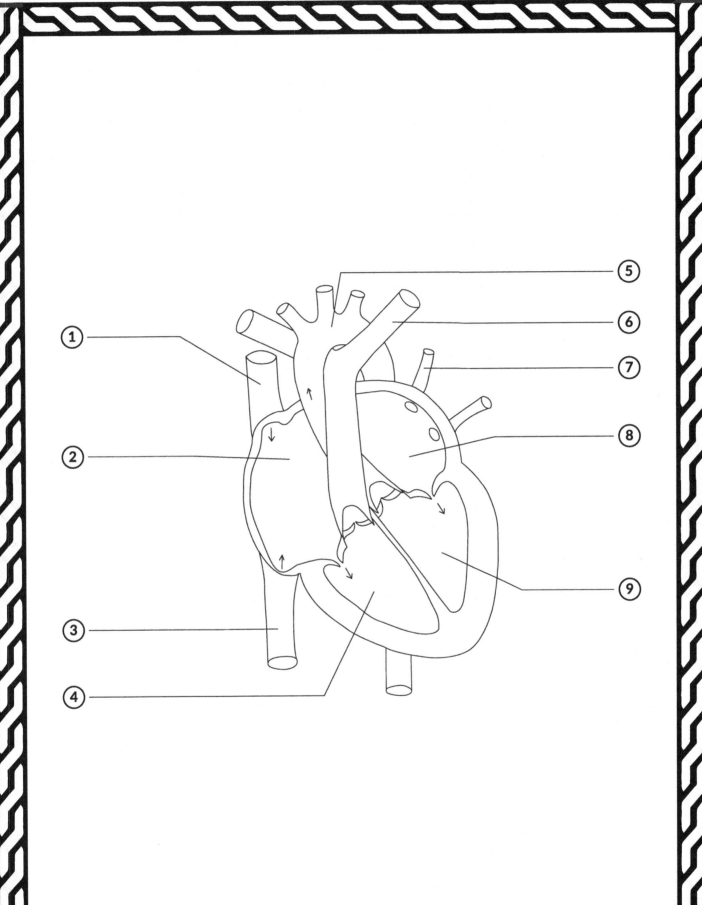

- - Answer - -

(1). Superior Vena Cava

(2). Right Atrium

(3). Inferior Vena Cava

(4). Right Ventricle

(5). Aorta

(6). Pulmonary Artery

(7). Pulmonary Vein

(8). Left Atrium

(9). Left Ventricle

Lower Pressure   Higher Pressure

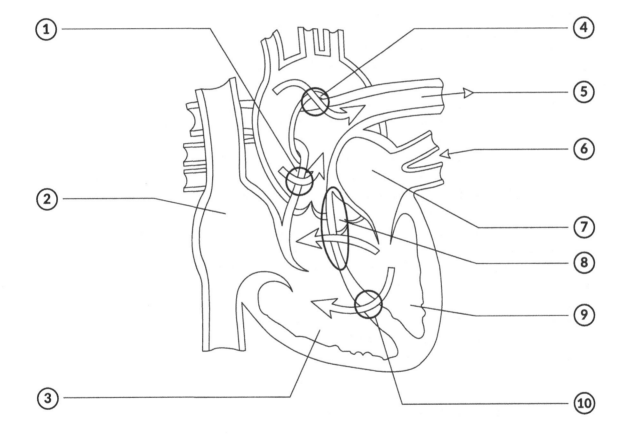

- - Answer - -

(1). Aorto-Pulmonary Window

(2). Right Atrium

(3). Right Ventricle

(4). Persistent Ductus Arteriosus

(5). Increased Flow To Lungs

(6). Increased Return To Left Atrium

(7). Left Atrium

(8). Atrio-Ventricular Septal Defect

(9). Left Ventricle

(10). Ventricular Septal Defect

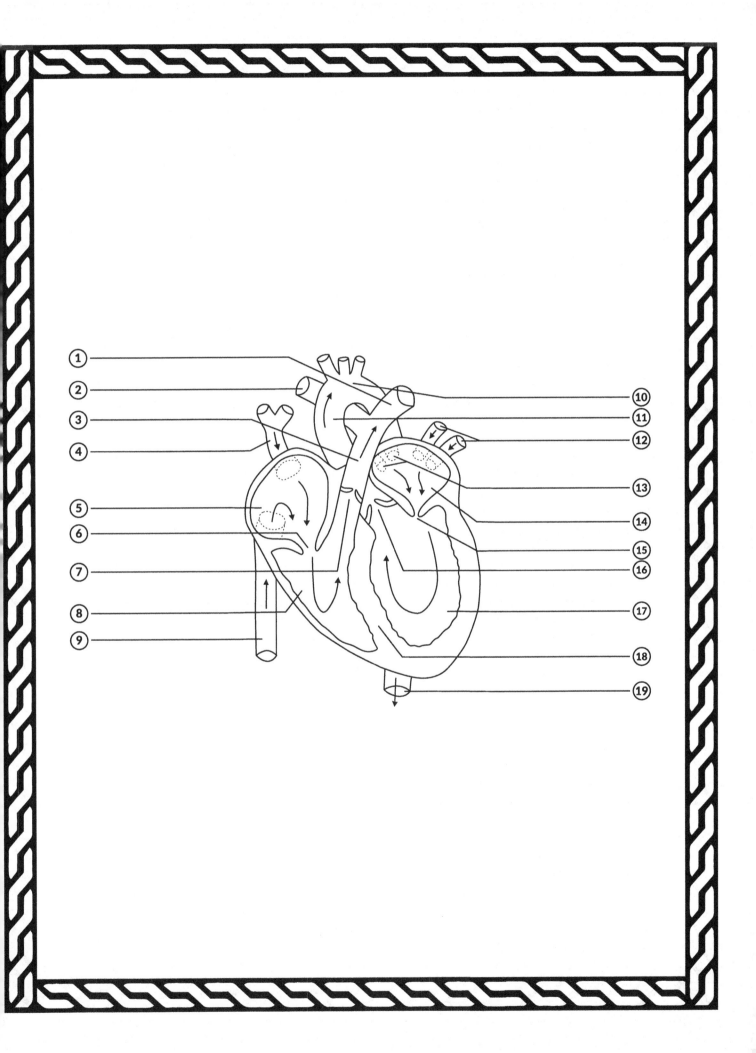

- - Answer - -

(1). Left Pulmonary Artery

(2). Right Pulmonary Artery

(3). Pulmonary Trunk

(4). Superior Vena Cava

(5). Right Atrium

(6). Right AV Valve

(7). Pulmonary Semilunar Valve

(8). Right Ventricle

(9). Inferior Vena Cava

(10). Aortic Arch

(11). Aorta

(12). Left Pulmonary Veins

(13). Right Pulmonary Veins

(14). Left Atrium

(15). Left AV Valve

(16). Aortic Semilunar Valve

(17). Left Ventricle

(18). Interventricular Septum

(19). Descending Aorta

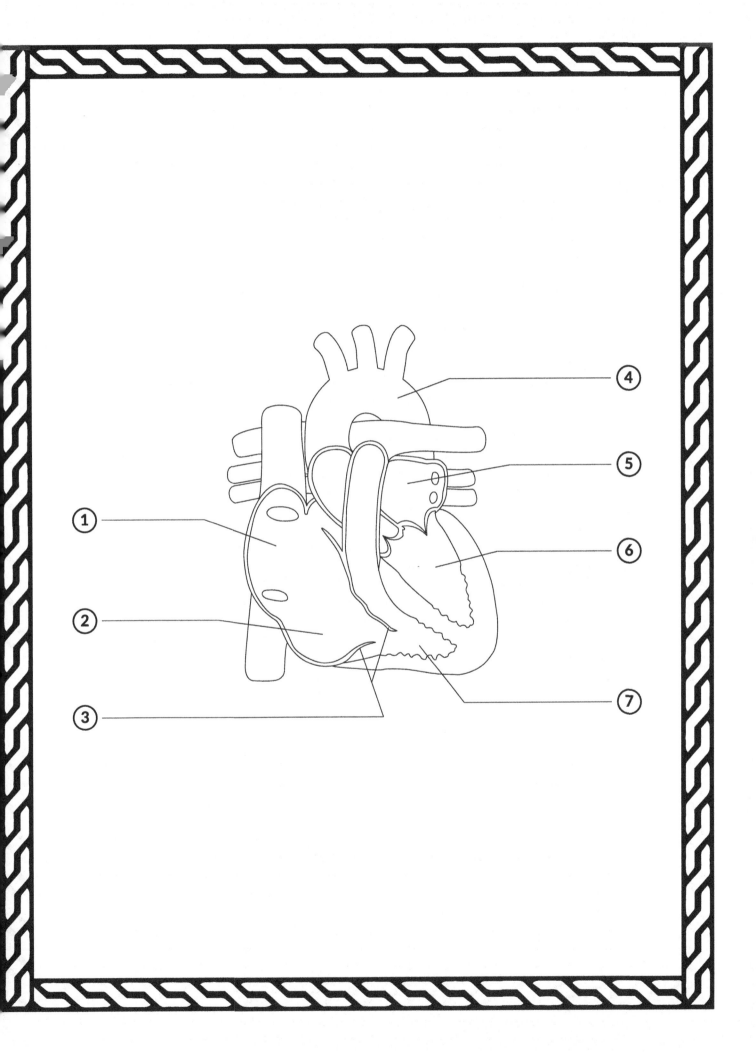

- - Answer - -

(1). Right Atrium

(2). Right Ventricle (Dilated Atrialized Portion)

(3). Abnormal Tricuspid Valve

(4). Aorta

(5). Left Atrium

(6). Left Ventricle

(7). Right Ventricle (Muscular Portion)

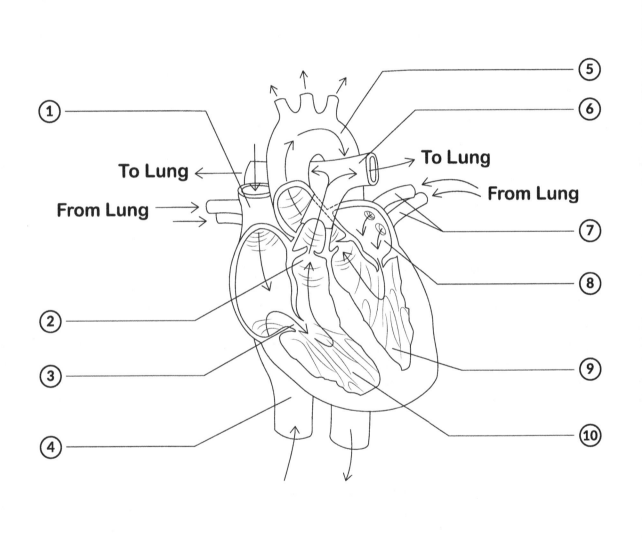

To Lung

From Lung

To Lung

From Lung

① ② ③ ④ ⑤ ⑥ ⑦ ⑧ ⑨ ⑩

- - Answer - -

(1). Superior Vena Cava

(2). Pulmonary Valve

(3). Atrioventricular Valve

(4). Inferior Vena Cava

(5). Aorta

(6). Pulmonary Artery

(7). Pulmonary Vein

(8). Left Atrium

(9). Left Ventricle

(10). Right Ventricle

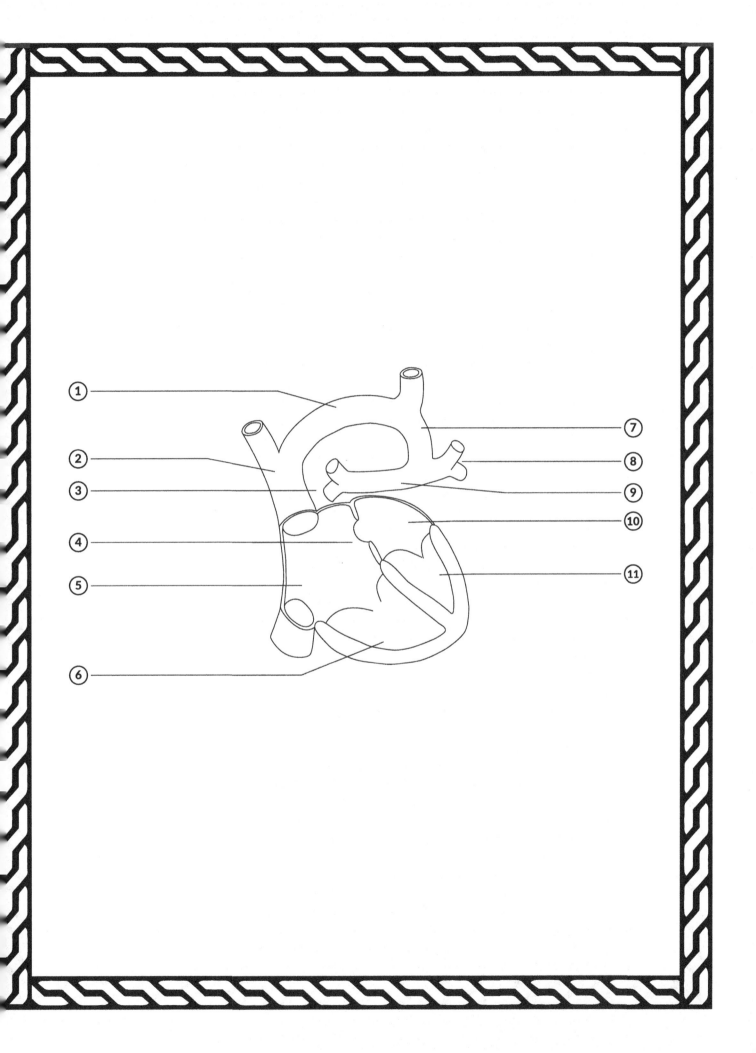

- - Answer - -

(1). Innominate Vein

(2). Superior Vena Cava

(3). Right Pulmonary Vein

(4). Atrial Septal Defect

(5). Right Atrium

(6). Right Ventricle

(7). Vertical Vein

(8). Left Pulmonary Vein

(9). Common Vein

(10). Left Atrium

(11). Left Ventricle

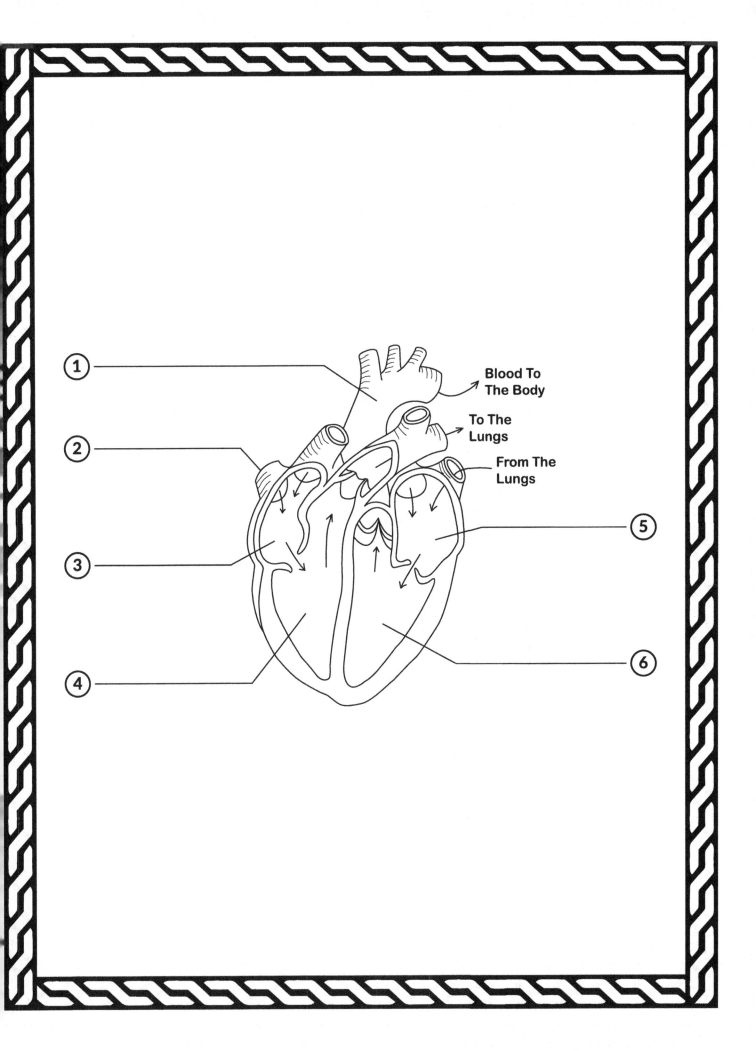

Blood To
The Body

To The
Lungs

From The
Lungs

- - Answer - -

(1). Aorta

(2). Blood From The Body

(3). Right Auricle

(4). Right Ventricle

(5). Left Auricle

(6). Left Ventricle

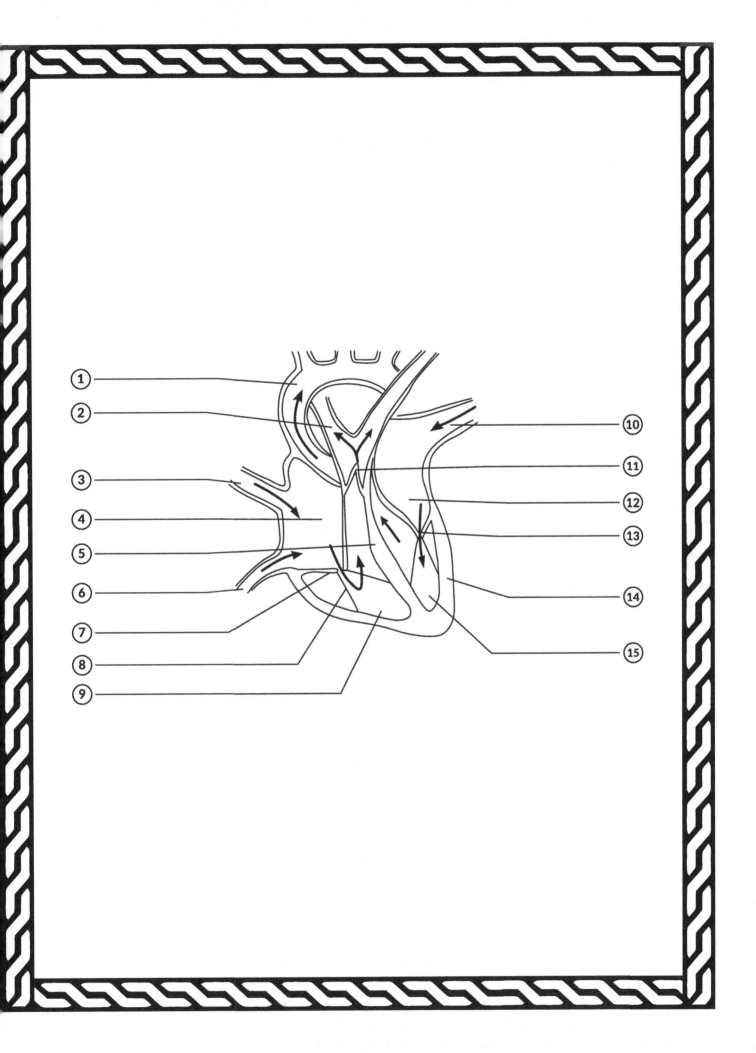

- - Answer - -

(1). Aorta

(2). Pulmonary Artery

(3). Vena Cava

(4). Right Atrium

(5). Septum

(6). Vena Cava

(7). Tricuspid Valve

(8). Tendon

(9). Right Ventricle

(10). Pulmonary Vein

(11). Semi-lunar Valve

(12). Left Atrium

(13). Bicuspid Valve

(14). Thick Wall On Left

(15). Left Ventricle

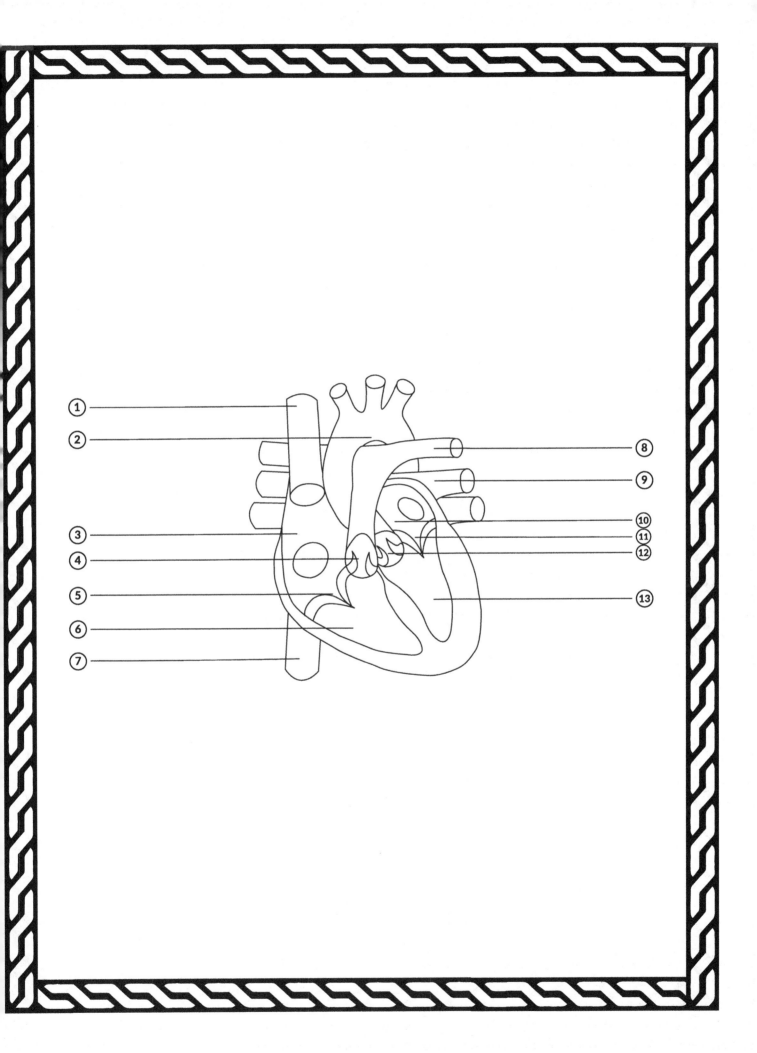

- - Answer - -

(1). Superior Vena Cava

(2). Aorta

(3). Right Atrium

(4). Pulmonary Valve

(5). Tricuspid Valve

(6). Right Ventricle

(7). Interior Vena Cava

(8). Pulmonary Artery

(9). Pulmonary Vein

(10). Left Atrium

(11). Mitral Valve

(12). Aortic Valve

(13). Left Ventricle

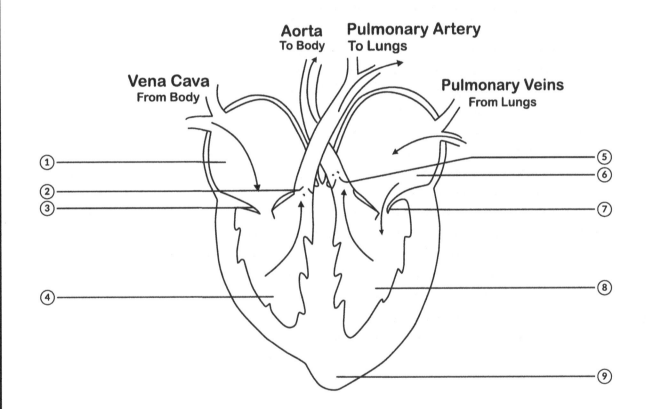

Vena Cava
From Body

Aorta
To Body

Pulmonary Artery
To Lungs

Pulmonary Veins
From Lungs

① ② ③ ④ ⑤ ⑥ ⑦ ⑧ ⑨

- - Answer - -

(1). Right Atrium

(2). Pulmonary Valve

(3). Tricuspid Valve

(4). Right Ventricle

(5). Aortic Valve

(6). Left Atrium

(7). Mitral Valve Bicuspid Valve

(8). Left Ventricle

(9). Thick Cardiac Muscle

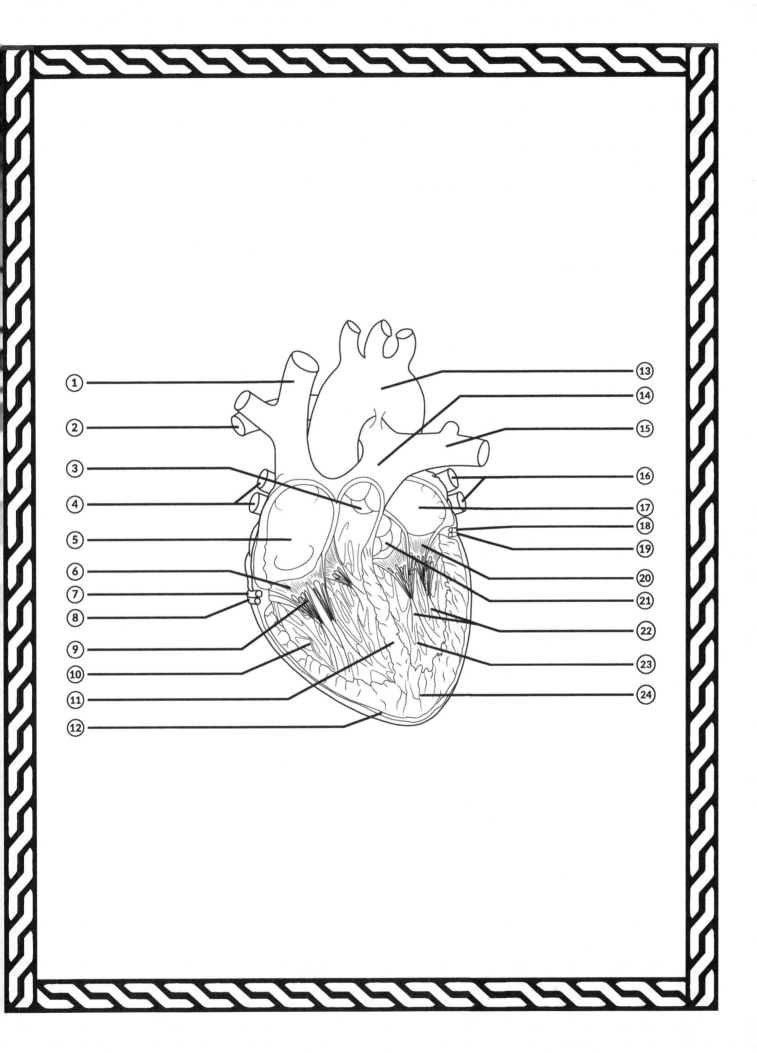

- - Answer - -

(1). Superior Vena Cava

(2). Right Pulmonary Artery

(3). Pulmonary Semilunar Valve

(4). Right Pulmonary Veins

(5). Right Atrium

(6). Tricuspid Valve

(7). Right Coronary Artery

(8). Small Cardiac Vein

(9). Chordae Tendineae

(10). Right Ventricle

(11). Interventricular Septum

(12). Adipose Tissue

(13). Aorta

(14). Pulmonary Trunk

(15). Left Pulmonary Artery

(16). Left Pulmonary Veins

(17). Left Atrium

(18). Left Coronary Artery

(19). Great Cardiac Vein

(20). Mitral Valve

(21). Aortic Semilunar Valve

(22). Papillary Muscle

(23). Left Ventricle

(24). Miocardium

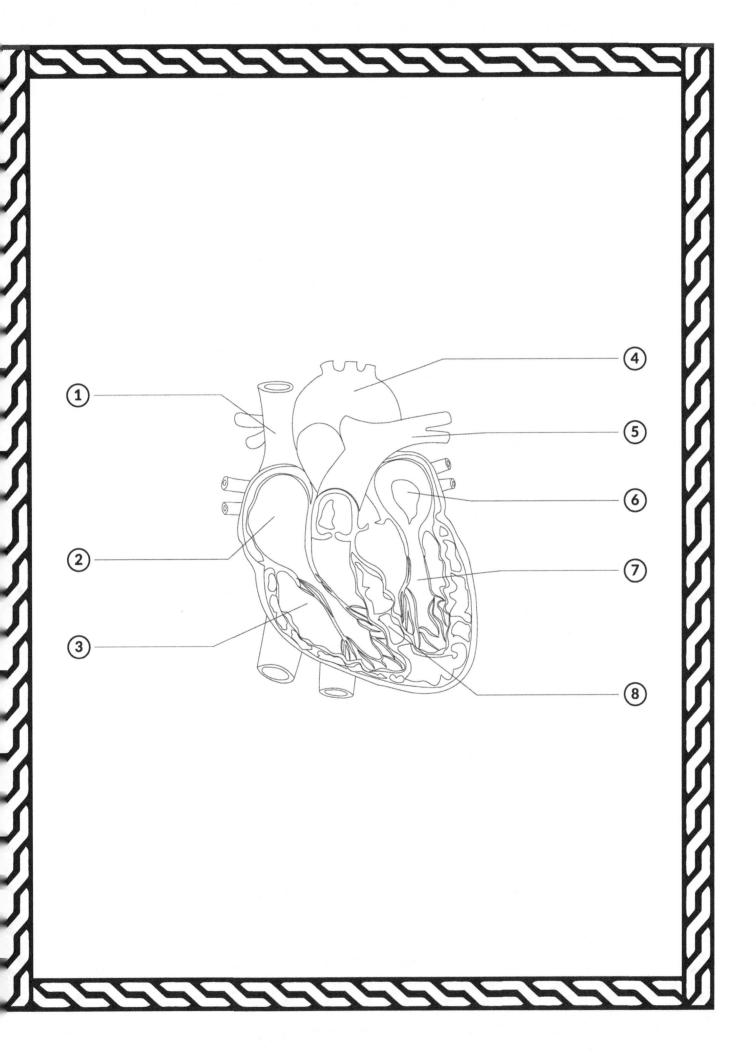

- - Answer - -

(1). Superior Vena Cava

(2). Right Atrium

(3). Right Ventricle

(4). Aorta

(5). Pulmonary Artery

(6). Left Atrium

(7). Left Ventricle

(8). Interventricular Septum

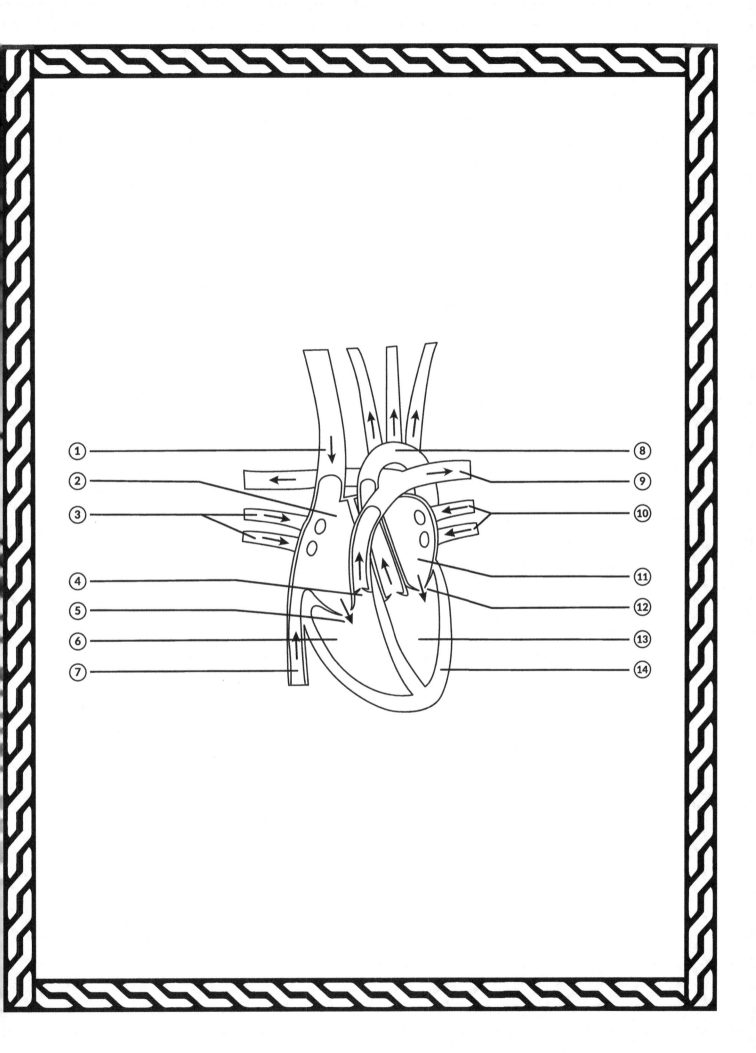

① ② ③ ④ ⑤ ⑥ ⑦ ⑧ ⑨ ⑩ ⑪ ⑫ ⑬ ⑭

- - Answer - -

(1). Superior Vena Cava

(2). Right Atrium

(3). Pulmonary Veins

(4). Pulmonary Valve

(5). Tricuspid Valve

(6). Right Ventricle

(7). Inferior Vena Cava

(8). Aorta

(9). Pulmonary Artery

(10). Pulmonary Veins

(11). Left Atrium

(12). Mitral Valve

(13). Left Ventricle

(14). Cardiac Muscle

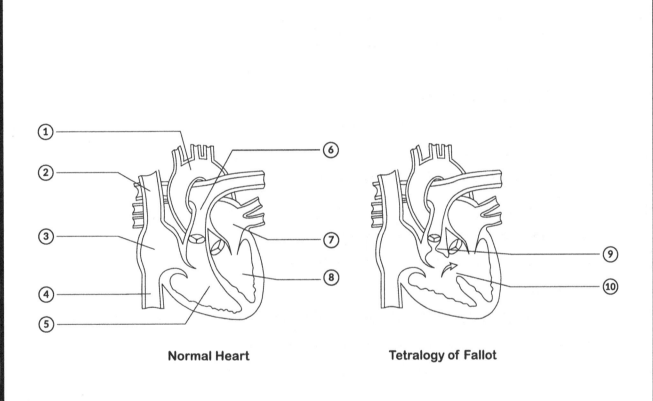

Normal Heart

Tetralogy of Fallot

- - Answer - -

(1). Aorta

(2). Superior Vena Cava

(3). Right Atrium

(4). Inferior Vena Cava

(5). Right Ventricle

(6). Pulmonary Artery

(7). Left Atrium

(8). Left Ventricle

(9). Narrowing of The Pulmonary Valve

(10). Ventricular Septal Defect

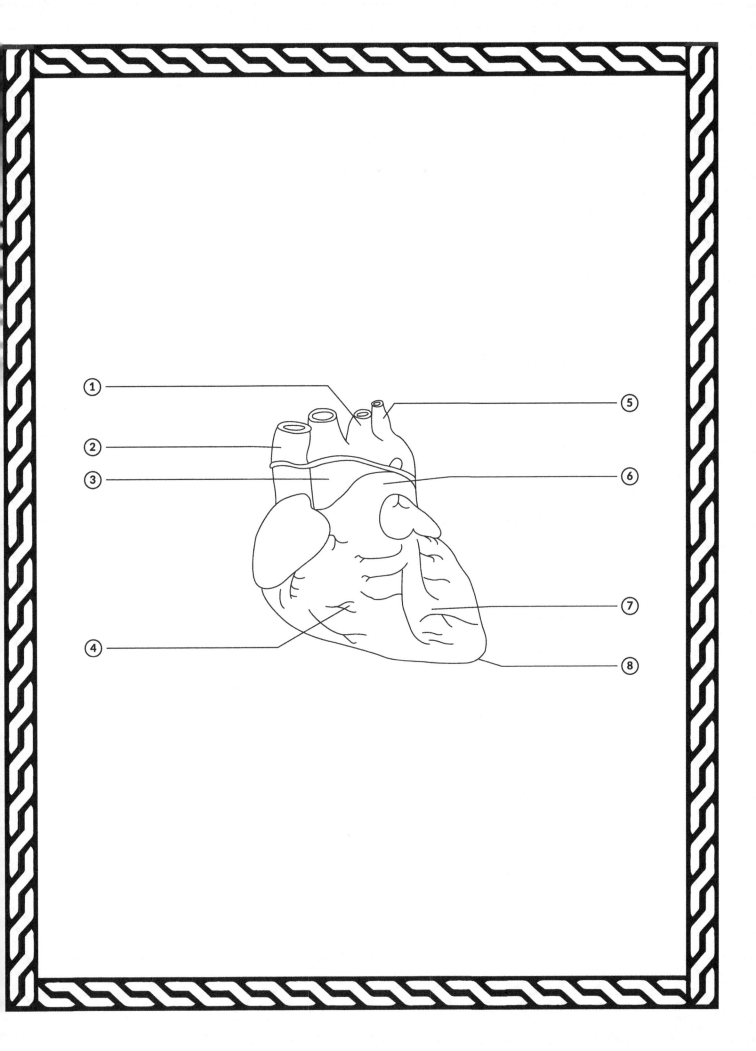

- - Answer - -

(1). Left Common Carotid Artery

(2). Superior Vena Cava

(3). Aorta

(4). Right Ventricle

(5). Left Subclavian Artery

(6). Pulmonary artery

(7). Left Ventricle

(8). Apex

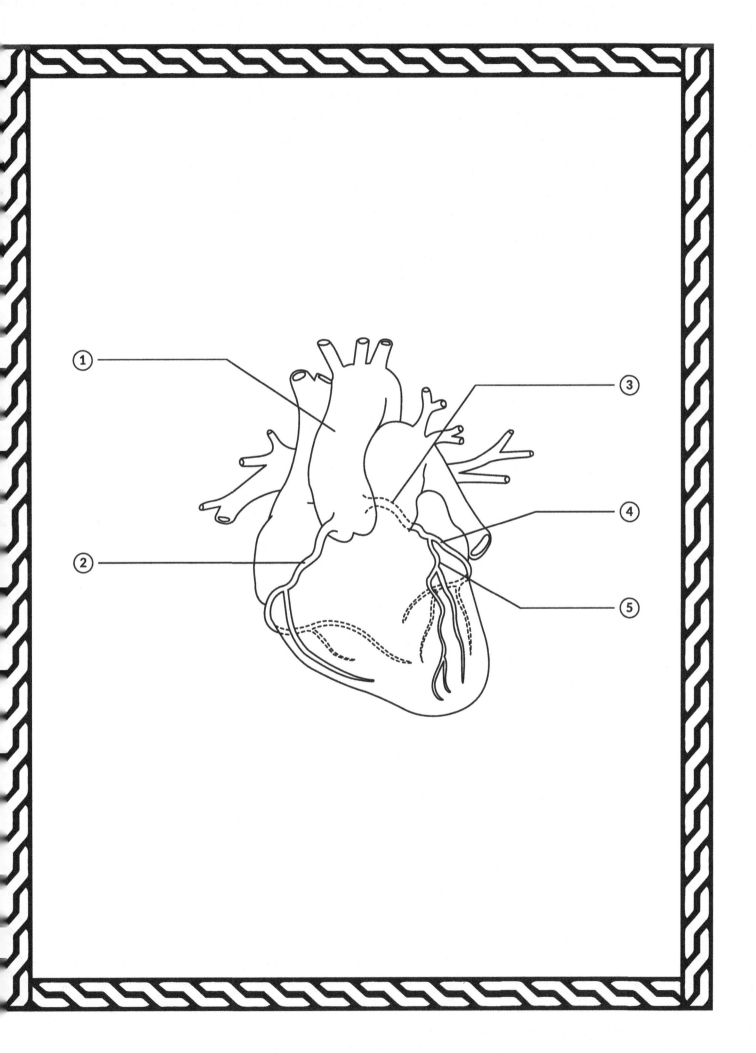

- - Answer - -

(1). Aorta

(2). Right Coronary Artery

(3). Left Coronary Artery

(4). Circumflex Artery

(5). Left Anterior Descending Artery

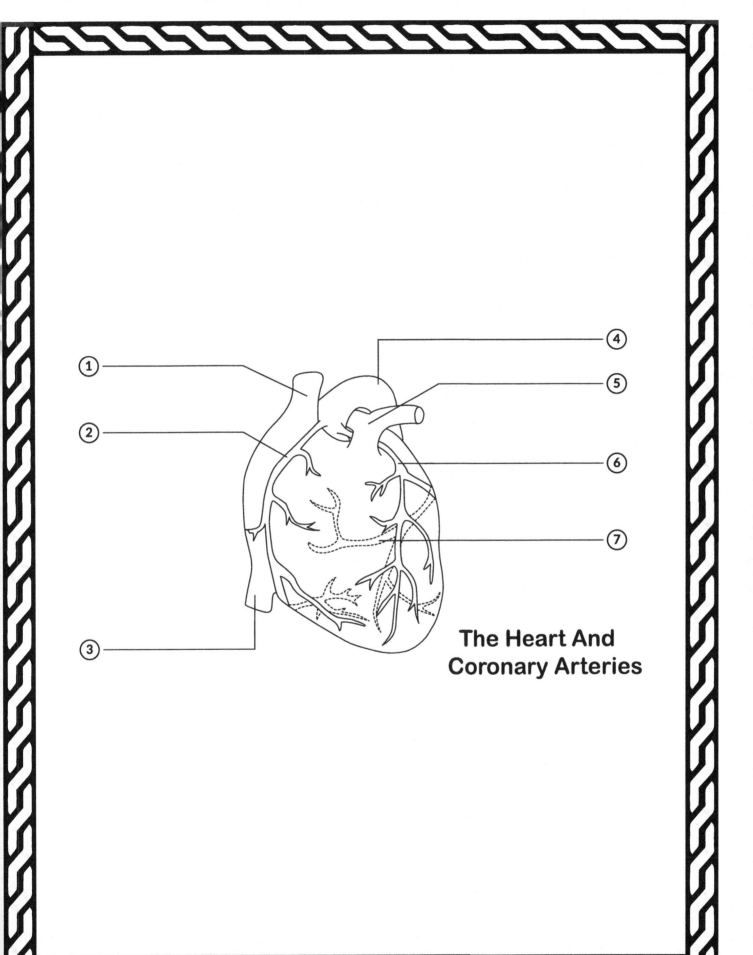

The Heart And Coronary Arteries

- - Answer - -

(1). Superior Vena Cava

(2). Right Coronary Artery

(3). Inferior Vena Cava

(4). Aorta

(5). Pulmonary Arteries

(6). Left Coronary Artery

(7). Circumflex Branch of Left Coronary Artery

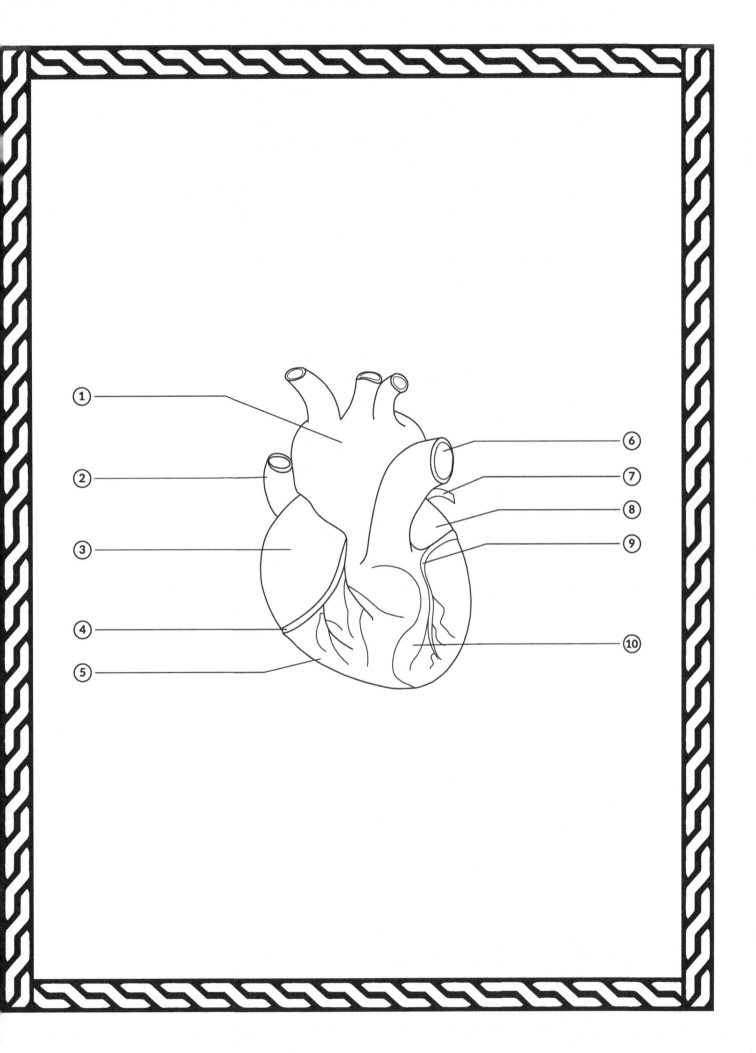

- - Answer - -

(1). Aorta

(2). Superior Vena Cava

(3). Right Atrium

(4). Right Coronary Artery

(5). Right Ventricle

(6). Pulmonary Artery

(7). Pulmonary Vein

(8). Left Atrium

(9). Left Coronary Artery

(10). Left Ventricle

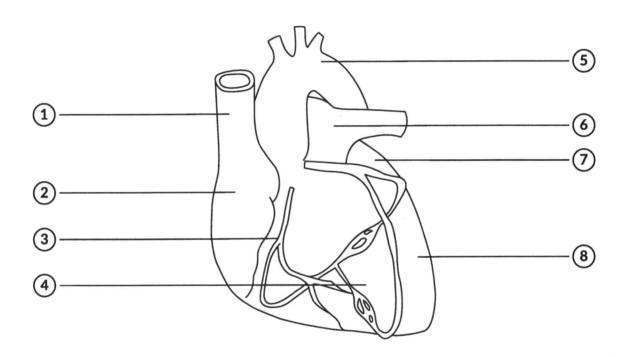

External Structure of Human Heart

- - Answer - -

(1). Superior Vena Cava

(2). Right Atrium

(3). Coronary Artery

(4). Right Ventricle

(5). Aorta

(6). Pulmonary Artery

(7). Left Atrium

(8). Left Ventricle

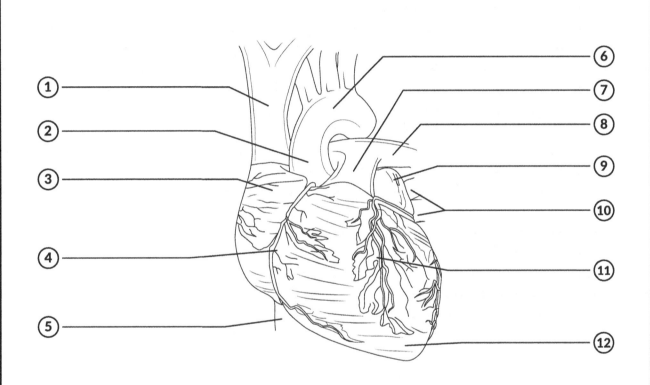

Superficial Heart Anatomy (Anterior)

- - Answer - -

(1). Superior Vena Cava

(2). Ascending Aorta

(3). Auricle of Right Atrium

(4). Fat And Vessels In Coronary Sulcus

(5). Inferior Vena Cava

(6). Arch of Aorta

(7). Pulmonary Trunk

(8). Left Pulmonary Artery

(9). Auricle of Left Atrium

(10). Left Pulmonary Veins

(11). Fat And Vessels In Anterior Interventricular Sulcus

(12). Apex of Heart

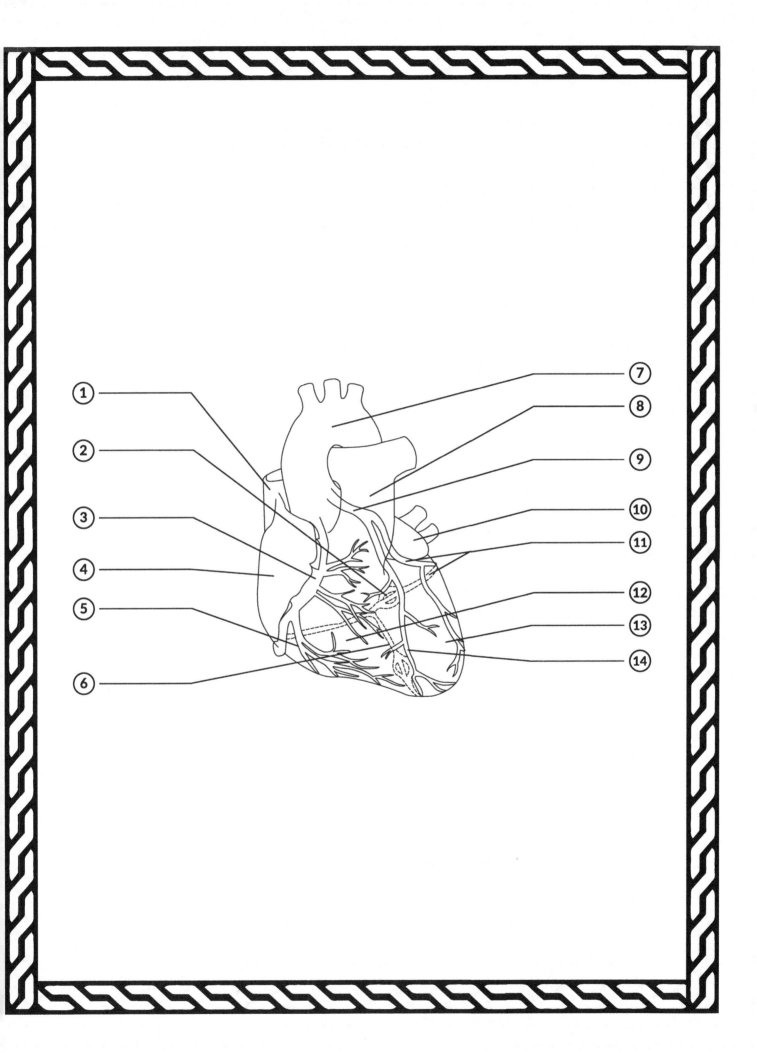

- - Answer - -

(1). Superior Vena Cava

(2). Anastomosis (Junction Of Vessels)

(3). Right Coronary Artery

(4). Right Atrium

(5). Marginal Artery

(6). Posterior Interventricular Artery

(7). Aorta

(8). Pulmonary Trunk

(9). Left Coronary Artery

(10). Left Atrium

(11). Circumflex Artery

(12). Right Ventricle

(13). Left Ventricle

(14). Anterior Interventricular Artery

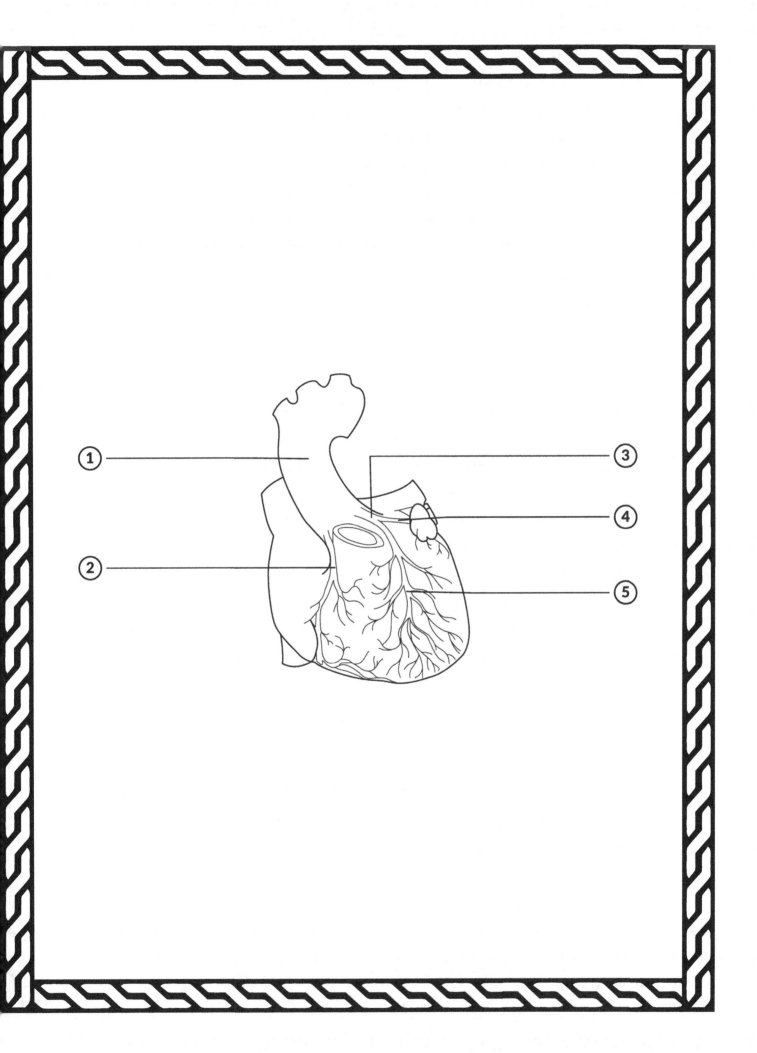

- - Answer - -

(1). Aorta

(2). Right Coronary Artery

(3). Left Main Coronary Artery

(4). Circumflex Branch

(5). Anterior Descending Branch